design, Cut & Shape

HAZEL KING

www.heinemann.co.uk
Visit our website to find out more information about Heinemann Library books.

To order:
 Phone 44 (0) 1865 888066
 Send a fax to 44 (0) 1865 314091
Visit the Heinemann Bookshop at www.heinemann.co.uk to browse our catalogue
and order online.

First published in Great Britain by Heinemann Library,
Halley Court, Jordan Hill, Oxford OX2 8EJ,
a division of Reed Educational and Professional Publishing Ltd.
Heinemann is a registered trademark of Reed Educational & Professional Publishing Limited.

OXFORD MELBOURNE AUCKLAND
JOHANNESBURG BLANTYRE GABORONE
IBADAN PORTSMOUTH NH (USA) CHICAGO

Designed by AMR
Illustrations by Paul Beebee at Beehive Illustration and Art Construction
Originated by Ambassador Litho Ltd
Printed in Hong Kong/China

04 03 02 01 00
10 9 8 7 6 5 4 3 2 1

ISBN 0 431 10563 4

British Library Cataloguing in Publication Data
King, Hazel
  Design cut & shape. – (Trends in textile technology)
  1.Costume design – Juvenile literature 2.Fashion – Juvenile
  literature
  I.Title
  646.3

Acknowledgements
The Publishers would like to thank the following for permission to reproduce photographs:
Brother: p20, 23; Eye Ubiquitous: Yioros Nikiteas p22; Gerber Technology: p6, 17, 19; Heinemann:
G Boden pp5, 8, 13, 14, 27, 37, 42; Katherine Goodison p31; Rex Features: J Sutton Hibbert p29;
Science Photo Library: Dr Jeremy Burgess p41; Tony Stone Images: Andy Sacks p39.

Cover photograph reproduced with permission of Big Pictures.

Our thanks to Andy Rumsby for his comments in the preparation of this book.

Every effort has been made to contact copyright holders of any material reproduced in this book.
Any omissions will be rectified in subsequent printings if notice is given to the Publisher.

Any words appearing in the text in bold, **like this**, are explained in the glossary.

contents

inspired ideas   4

computer-aided design   6

cut and shape   8

measuring up   10

equipped for the job   12

commercial patterns   14

industrial pattern making   16

cutting and costing   18

sewing up   20

industrial sewing   22

fabric joining   24

moulding fabric   26

shaping fabric   28

couture millinery   30

sleeve shapes   32

collars and cuffs   34

fasten up   36

zip it up – a case study   38

fastenings from nature   40

textile project: hat   42

resources   44

glossary   46

index   48

inspired ideas

Ideas for new items made of textiles do not appear out of thin air! Usually a **need** has been identified through extensive research and the designer is responding to that need.

Textile designers are usually given a **design brief** which outlines the item to be designed, its end use and the target market. As well as being creative, a designer must have a sound knowledge of fibres, yarns, fabrics, manufacturing techniques and costs. Very often, the ball is set rolling when a **client**, who may be an individual or a company, asks a designer or design team to fulfil the need for a new textile item or items.

Design plans

Once the design brief has been set, a design plan can help to organize the planning. It is essential to meet the deadline for a project, whether you are working for a client or producing coursework at school, so planning ahead can help with this. All design-and-make work involves evaluation and reassessment, so the plan may need adjusting from time to time. The design plan outlines the steps to be followed when designing and making a textile item or items, and sets dates for completion for each one. An example is shown below.

A Design Plan

Task	Details	Completion date
Design brief	Consult with client; discuss requirement; discuss considerations and limitations of the brief; prepare specification	
Design plan	Plan time allowed for each aspect of task; decide on criteria for evaluation	
Design ideas	Research and investigate possible solutions to problem; disassemble similar products; record ideas; make mock-ups/models	
Developed ideas	Select and test best ideas; consult with client; produce working drawings and plans; present final idea	
Work plan	Outline plan for production including pattern, fabric cutting, joining, neatening seams, fastenings, embellishment	
Evaluation	Designer evaluation; client evaluation; user evaluation	

Storyboards can help designers to create a 'picture' for design ideas. ▶

Generating ideas

When designers investigate a design brief it is important that they sketch any ideas and save them to help generate ideas for the final solution. They should **annotate** sketches with notes explaining the thinking behind them or the type of fabric etc. They can collect swatches (samples) of fabric or yarn and practise different processes or techniques. They can also assess and even **disassemble** similar products to find out the materials and processes used in their manufacture. All of this experimentation and investigation helps to ensure the final product is successful and meets a specific need. They may consult other designers, consumers and the client during this stage.

Presenting ideas

When designers present an idea they use a combination of drawings, text and computer-generated images. Designing may involve drawing garments, accessories, furnishings and other household items. Design ideas for garments and accessories can be drawn on their own or as they would be worn by people from the consumer target group. For furnishings, designers are likely to draw in background furniture or a window frame, to show the overall effect. They may show other household items in their correct setting or on their own.

To help create a 'picture' for design ideas designers often use **storyboards**, which show the overall image of the new product. These are often used to evaluate designs as they are developing or as a way of presenting the final solution to the client.

Working drawings

A working drawing is one that assists in the making of the product, so it must show all the elements and details of the design. If the item is a garment, the cut, shape and proportion of the clothes must be very clear, and details such as types of seam, fastenings, decorations etc. properly labelled. The drawings often have fabric and colour swatches attached to them and different views – the back, sides, top etc. – have to be clearly visible.

Computer-aided design

Many designers use computers for their design work, either to create the whole design or to help with certain aspects of it. Design software enables images to be drawn and manipulated on screen in two or three dimensions. The designer can experiment with different **colourways** and can obtain a print-out of the design.

computer-aided design

The computer has had a huge impact on almost every aspect of our lives in recent years and textiles are no exception. The influence of the computer begins at the textile design stage and continues through manufacturing and marketing to the sale of goods. **Computer-aided design** (CAD) has enabled designers to produce exciting new fabrics and textile items easily and efficiently, but this area of creativity can be controversial. Some argue that a computer cannot be creative because its calculations are based on computing information. Nonetheless, there is no doubt that it can be used as a tool to produce original creations.

Apple Macintosh

The computer company Apple Macintosh first introduced computers into the world of textile design by producing user-friendly programs as opposed to those that require a great deal of computer literacy. Software programs began to offer tools related specifically to textile design, enabling the designer to create a three-dimensional image.

Today, textile designers can use sophisticated techniques to reproduce computerized effects on to fabric. For example, reactive inks and special printers help to recreate a three-dimensional quality, and holographic foils may be added to textiles during the printing process. By carefully selecting colours, patterns can appear in the foreground while others fade into the background.

Surface decoration

Computer-aided design allows complex patterns to be completed relatively quickly. Colour schemes can be altered with the click of a button rather than a re-modelling of the entire design. However, despite the fact that designs are computer-generated, they are still as unique as those sketched by hand. Every designer will have their own way of using a computer and may combine freehand drawing with computer-aided design.

▼ *Computers have revolutionized textile design. Sophisticated effects can be produced quickly and easily using CAD packages.*

Testing new designs

Computer-aided design systems are now being developed to test new designs. For example, the Advanced Technology Unit at Ove Arup and Partners in London has developed software for crash-testing vehicles. The software system analyses the effect of a crash on the people in the vehicle, the type of injuries sustained and the effectiveness of airbags and seatbelts. The real advantage of simulating a crash in this way is that designs can be tested before they reach the **prototype** stage, saving both time and money. Safety testing of this sort is important for many textile items too - for example, testing the flammability of a firefighter's uniform or children's nightwear.

Virtual reality

The technology we now know as **virtual reality** was initiated by research into flight simulation carried out by NASA, the National Aeronautics and Space Administration in the USA. To experience virtual reality using a computer, you wear a helmet that incorporates a screen in front of your eyes. In fact there are two screens, but they are so close together you cannot detect a division between them. The computer recreates an image on the screen and when your head moves, the image adjusts accordingly, giving you the illusion that what you see in front of you is actually there, as if you didn't have a helmet on at all. The impression of reality is enhanced by special gloves that enable you to 'touch' and 'move' objects within the image.

Technology of the future

Highly technical industries such as NASA have always been involved in the development of performance fibres and fabrics, but perhaps in the future we will all be wearing clothes that perform very specific functions. For example, in 1995 Daniel Cooper designed a chameleon jacket that is able to monitor and protect the wearer from environmental pollution. The front panels are made from nylon and in-built detectors monitor levels of nitrogen oxide, sulphur dioxide and ozone. When there is little or no pollution the jacket is blue and when pollution levels are high it changes to orange. The jacket includes a Neoprene face mask that you can wear during times of high pollution. The air you inhale is filtered as it passes through a layer of charcoal-impregnated felt.

Virtual gloves

An example of an early virtual glove was the Dataglove developed in the 1980s. It was made from a Lycra®-based fabric which allowed a great deal of flexibility. It was fitted with specially treated optical fibres running along the fingers, which sent signals to a central processor. The glove could monitor the ten finger joints and the position of the hand. Another virtual glove, the PowerGlove, was later developed by Mattel Toy Company for their Nintendo home video games. In this instance, moulded plastic was teamed up with a Lycra®-based fabric to make the glove more cost-effective.

Although still rather costly today, virtual gloves may eventually provide an alternative way for designers to design using the computer.

cut and shape

From 2-D to 3-D

The creation of many textile items is dependent upon changing a flat fabric into a three-dimensional form. Consider for a moment a range of products made from material: a teddy bear, a baseball cap, a shirt, a pencil case, canvas shoes – they all started out as a flat piece of fabric. Even knitted items made from a single yarn can be shaped during the knitting process so they become three-dimensional. Fabric is an incredibly versatile material to use when designing and making items because it can be manipulated in many ways to produce an array of different shapes and forms.

Forming a shape

Everything has shape or form. Generally speaking, shape refers to two-dimensional items and form refers to three-dimensional ones. When a fabric is cut into specific shapes, the shapes may be joined together to create an end-product which has form. The way fabric is cut is an extremely important process in the creation of textile items.

Disassembly

Disassembly is a useful way to understand how a textile item is made. If a product is unpicked it reveals the shape of each piece of fabric used in its construction. It will also show the number of pieces used, the construction techniques and it is possible to estimate the total amount of fabric required. It is not always possible to disassemble an item due to its cost or sentimental value. In this case the item must be carefully analysed without actually undoing the stitching; the type of fabric and components can be identified as well as seams and stitches. A person experienced in textile construction will also be able to work out the order in which the pieces were put together during the making.

Disassembly is an expensive way of analysing textile items because it usually means the product is destroyed in the process, particularly if the fibre content is revealed with burning tests. However, it is a very useful way for textile manufacturers or designers to evaluate similar products and find out more about items already on the market. It is also crucial when textiles are tested to ensure they are meeting their legal requirements.

The pieces of fabric used to create these 3-D items were all carefully cut, shaped and joined together.

Taking things apart

If you have an old textile item at home that is no longer required, try the following disassembly activity to see what you can find out from it. If possible, use an item that you would like to make one day because this will help you to understand how it is made.

Resources
- an old textile item (shirt, soft toy etc.) which you are sure is no longer needed
- small pair of sharp scissors
- notepad and pen
- camera, if possible, to photograph each stage of the disassembly.

Method

1 Look for a label as this will tell you what the fabric(s) is. If there is no label see if you can identify the fabric type for yourself; knowing how the item is washed (if at all) should help with this.

2 Look carefully at the whole item. Are there any buttons or decorations which were added at the end of construction that you can remove first? If not, which seam do you think was the last to be sewn? This will be the one you can unpick first.

3 Cut the stitches carefully. Make notes about what you have done.

4 Continue unpicking the item carefully and note down each piece or section. Aim to undo the item in the *reverse* order of its construction.

5 When your item is disassembled lay each piece out flat. Look at the shape of the pieces.

If you want to make the item using a new fabric you could use the disassembled pieces and your notes to reconstruct a new item! (Don't forget seams are usually trimmed after sewing, so you will need to allow a little extra fabric - 10mm - for every seam.)

Creating shapes

The human body has many bumps and lumps that must be taken into consideration if clothes are to fit perfectly; in the same way, items such as fabric-covered seats and chairs must be smooth and wrinkle-free. There are many techniques that can be employed to shape and form textile items. Cutting fabric into particular shapes and sewing the pieces together has already been mentioned but there are other ways to create curves. For example, darts, gathers and pleats are all used in the manipulation of fabric. Collars and cuffs provide a close fit in specific areas of some garments. Fastenings can be used where an item needs a tight fit and fabric can be moulded using steam as in the hat industry. All of these techniques will be explored further in the pages that follow.

measuring up

Measuring is an important aspect of the design-and-make process in textiles. It is essential that all measurements are accurate. If a textile product is to fit together neatly during construction, precise measurements must be taken during the designing and planning stages. In the manufacture of a garment for a specific person, a series of measurements of their body are made. The measuring should reflect the actual body measurements (not too tight or too loose) rather than the measurements for the garment itself. From these body measurements, **block patterns** can be made which can be adapted for specific clothing designs.

Body measurements

The diagrams below show the different measurements of the body that are used in tailoring clothes.

1 Chest – around body, above bust and under arms
2 Bust – around body and fullest part of bust
3 Waist – around body at point where body naturally curves in
4 Hips – around body at fullest part of hip
5 Upper hips – around body and over hip bones
6 Back length – from nape (base of neck) to waistline (see above)
7 Front length – from base of throat to waistline
8 Back width – from one armhole edge to the other
9 Shoulder – from neck to shoulder edge
10 Body rise – when sitting; from waist to chair, measuring over hip
11 Inside leg – from crotch to ankle bone
12 Outside leg – from waist to ankle bone, measuring over hip
13 Neck to wrist – from neck to wrist, measuring over shoulder and straight arm
14 Under arm – under arm to wrist
15 Biceps – around upper arm at widest point
16 Wrist – around widest part of wrist
17 Elbow – around widest part of elbow with arm bent
18 Shoulder width – under armpit and over shoulder
19 Skirt length – from centre front of waist to length required

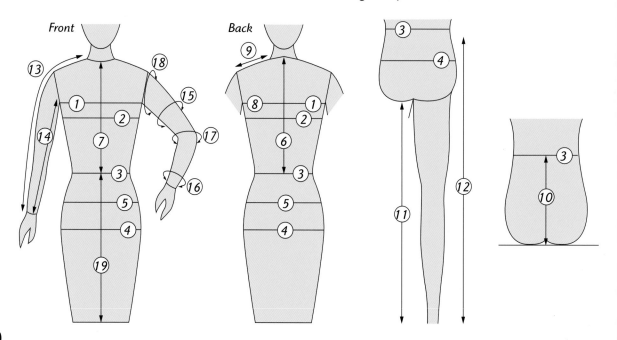

Pattern pieces

Someone making clothes uses body measurements and block patterns to make the pattern pieces of a garment. These are accurately shaped pieces that are used to transfer the shape of the clothing on to the fabric. They are also used to work out how much fabric is needed. The most economic use of fabric can be established by manipulating the pieces until they cover the fabric with the least amount of waste. In industry, this process is called lay planning, and the job is often done with the help of a computer (see page 16).

The changing shape of women

Evans, the company who own Dorothy Perkins, Principles and Racing Green, have decided to change their sizing system after carrying out a survey of the shape of women today. The survey revealed that British women are more pear-shaped than the current sizing system caters for. Evans have set a new standard which their suppliers are now going to use. The earlier 'ideal' female figure of 36-24-36 is now more like 36-28-38. However, some people feel changing a size 16 into a size 14 is encouraging people to be overweight. In the future, clothing may be given a colour-coded system rather than numerical labels.

Shapes and sizes

Clothes that are made at home or for **one-off production** such as **haute couture**, can be tailored to someone's exact measurements. However, when clothes need to be made on a large scale for **mass production**, the clothing industry uses standard sizes that have been created by the **British Standards Institute** (BSI). This means that size 12 jeans made by one manufacturer should be the same as size 12 jeans made by another. The BSI has to continually monitor the population to check whether average physical size is changing, and alter the standard sizes to accommodate any changes. Men's clothes are labelled with specific sizes, such as waist size for trousers and shorts. The current measurements for women are shown in the table below.

Standard women's sizes (cm)

	size 8	size 10	size 12	size 14	size 16
Bust	80	83	87	92	97
Waist	61	64	67	71	76
Hips	85	88	92	97	102
Back	40	40.5	41.5	42	42.5

Petite sizes are now quite common in many female clothes shops. The petite range caters for women who are shorter than 1.55m (5' 3").

equipped for the job

When you create items out of textiles at home or at school, you need to use various basic tools and pieces of equipment. The type of tools you need, of course, depends on your task. The following information is a guide to some of the basic items required and their function.

Cutting edge

There is a whole range of different types of scissors available; the most important for textile tasks are those that cut fabric. Fabric shears must have smooth cutting edges and should not be used on any other material, particularly paper, as this will blunt the blades. Fabric shears tend to be quite large and the handles are shaped so that they are relatively comfortable to use. You need paper shears for cutting paper patterns and, as the paper is only thin, they should be fairly slim with a sharp point. **Pinking shears** are useful but not essential for every textile task. The blades have a zig-zag edge and are used either when you need to add a decorative feature or reduce the risk of fraying on a seam. If you need to make buttonholes, you sew buttonhole stitches first and cut the hole afterwards. For this sort of cutting it is useful to have very sharp, small scissors that can be easily controlled to avoid cutting the stitching by mistake. Buttonhole shears are ideal for this purpose as they have an adjustable screw that can determine the length of the hole that needs to be cut.

A stitch cutter is useful for unpicking stitches, as it is specially shaped to get underneath the stitch and then cut it. Equally useful are snippers which are spring-loaded so you can trim threads or remove tacking stitches quickly and easily. If you are sewing embroidery stitches, small embroidery scissors are available for cutting the threads. Often they are decorative in themselves. Notchers are also useful if paper patterns show notches to mark the position of darts, pleats, seams etc. These notches have to be transferred to the fabric, and notchers mark the fabric by cutting a shape at the specific point.

To the point

There are a whole range of needle sizes. It is important to choose the most suitable one for the job in hand, although you also need to be comfortable with the needle; some are very tiny and difficult to see. The choice of needle usually depends on the fabric and thread as well as the actual stitches you will be making. Sewing needles are categorized according to their length and thickness using a numbering system. 'Betweens' is the name for standard length needles used for fine work. 'Sharps' is the name for longer length needles used for general sewing. Embroidery, tapestry and darning needles tend to be thicker than sewing needles, with longer and wider eyes because the threads used are more bulky.

Surprisingly, sewing pins do differ to a certain extent. They are made from steel but their length and thickness can vary depending on the make, and some have coloured, plastic heads. Although the plastic heads mean the pins are easy to see you should not use them if you are machining pinned fabric as the heads can get caught in the machine. If you are working with delicate fabrics you should use fine and sharp pins to avoid tearing the fibres; on thicker fabrics you may also need longer length pins.

Pressing matters

Ironing is crucial when you make textile items such as clothes, because pressing the garment during construction will help to give it a smooth, professional finish. It is important to set an electric iron to the correct temperature for the particular fabric you are working with, to avoid scorching it. Steam irons are particularly useful if you are making

pleats. An ironing board is obviously essential but other helpful items include a sleeve board, an ironing cushion and a moulded buck. A sleeve board is like a miniature ironing board, and as its name suggests is for pressing sleeves; the ironing cushion and moulded buck are for pressing areas of an item that are not flat – for example, an armhole seam.

Bits and pieces

Other items that can be helpful in the making of textile items include tape measures, rulers, **tailor's chalk**, thimbles, pin cushions, **tracing wheels** and a **mannequin**.

▼ *Some basic items that may be useful when creating textile products.*

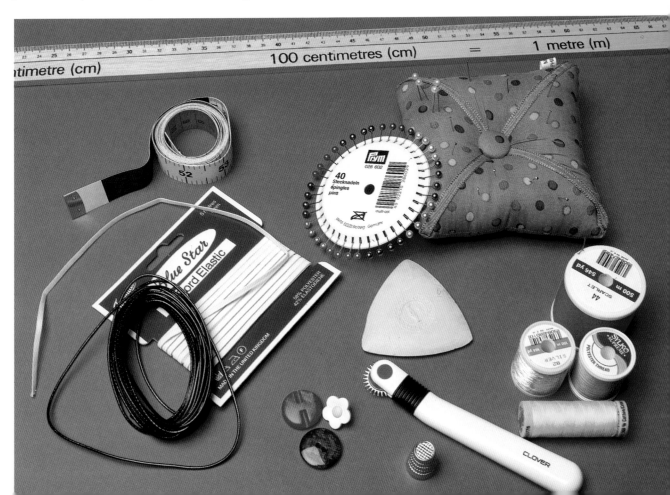

commercial patterns

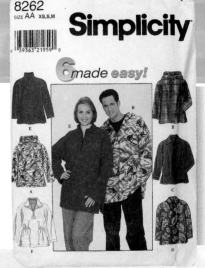

You can buy commercial patterns for making textile items at home. Shops selling fabrics usually have pattern books showing all the latest patterns from companies such as Style, Simplicity, and Vogue. Pattern books are updated every season in order to keep pace with changes in fashion, and patterns are available for all kinds of clothes. You can also buy patterns for making accessories, home furnishings and craft items.

A variety of fleece tops can be made using this commercial pattern. ▶

Choosing a pattern

Sewing patterns are sold in envelopes with a picture or photograph on the front showing the particular garment or item. You can see from the Simplicity envelope here that the photograph gives the most realistic representation of what the garment will look like. Detail such as the fabric type can also be seen more clearly. This particular pattern is size AA and is for a man or woman. Multi-size patterns are useful to the consumer and the manufacturer because they avoid having many patterns of different sizes.

Garment patterns often have different styles included in the same pattern. This fleece top pattern includes a hood, collar or stand-up collar as options; it can also be made with or without patch pockets, and it can have a draw-string waist. Each option is identified by a letter. The illustrations help you to visualize the top in different **colourways** and fabric patterns.

Helpful information

On the back of the envelope there will be more detailed information about the garment including sketches of the back views. The envelope shown here describes the top with all its variations and then gives suggestions about the most suitable fabrics to use. 'Notions' are all the extra items that will be needed to make the garment, such as fastenings and threads.

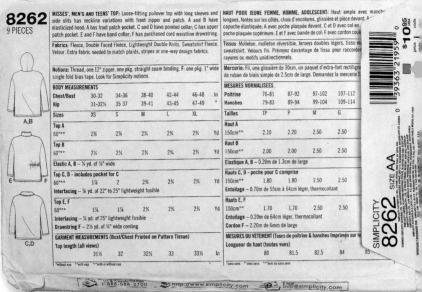

Deciding on fabric

Having decided which option you are going to make and the correct size, you need to find out how much fabric will be required. For example, for top D in size XS, you need $1\frac{7}{8}$ yard or 1.80 metres. (The English version gives imperial measurements, while the French version gives the metric equivalent.) However, this amount is for fabric of 60" or 150cm wide. As well as the fabric and notions, top D also needs $\frac{1}{4}$ yd/0.70m of **interfacing**.

At the bottom of the fabric information, you will see the words 'without **nap**', 'with nap' and 'with or without nap'. This indicates whether a matching pattern or fabric with a one-way design has been taken into account in the calculations. Fabric 'without nap' does not need matching but fabric 'with nap' does, and so more fabric will be needed.

Inside the envelope

A pattern contains printed pattern pieces and an instruction sheet. This shows all the pattern pieces in diagram form with numbers, so they can easily be identified. Once you have cut out all the necessary pattern pieces in the correct size, they can be laid out on the fabric using the 'Cutting Layouts' shown in the instructions. For top D, you have to cut out interfacing for the collar.

There are some general directions on commercial patterns to help you understand and interpret the pattern pieces and sewing directions. The diagrams here show the symbols on pattern pieces and their meaning:

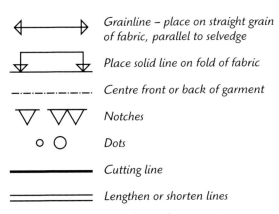

Grainline – place on straight grain of fabric, parallel to selvedge

Place solid line on fold of fabric

Centre front or back of garment

Notches

Dots

Cutting line

Lengthen or shorten lines

Seam allowance: 5/8" (1.5cm) unless otherwise stated is included but not printed on

This particular pattern also gives some tips for sewing fleece, as well as a key to help interpret the diagrams:

Fabric key

Right side	Wrong side	Interfacing	Lining

The construction of the top can then be followed step by step, using the instructions and diagrams provided:

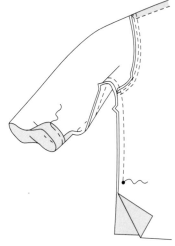

Pin front to back at entire underarm seam, matching armhole seams and large dots. Stitch seam from large dot to edge of sleeve. Back-stitch at large dot to reinforce seam.
Press up sleeve hem.
Stitch or zig-zag $\frac{1}{4}$" (6mm) from raw edge.

industrial pattern making

Patterns are a crucial part of the design-and-make process within textiles. A drawing may be translated into flat shapes using pattern pieces. When joined together the pieces make a three-dimensional form that reproduces a designer's sketch. The person who carries out this skilful task is called the pattern maker, and the work is done either manually or with the use of a computer. It requires a thorough knowledge of both design and construction.

Block patterns

In the clothing industry, there are standard **block patterns** for every type of garment and in all the standard sizes. Block patterns are adapted by the pattern maker to create the specific shape and detail the designer wants. Once the individual pattern pieces have been produced, a pattern draft is developed. This shows how the item will be put together, taking into account all the measurements. Once again, computers may be used to prepare pattern drafts quickly and easily and also to store the information so it is always available and may be adapted if necessary.

Grading

In **one-off production** a pattern will be produced to fit a specific **client**. However, during **mass production** and **batch production** the master pattern pieces must be altered so they can be used for a whole range of sizes. The process of increasing or decreasing the master pattern is known as grading. When this is done manually, a grading machine is used which grips the pattern

and moves it a precise distance. The new outline is then traced and so the process continues for other sizes. To grade a pattern using a computer, measurements are fed into the computer and the new sizes are automatically calculated.

Lay plans

The next step in the process is to work out how to arrange the pattern pieces to ensure the most economic use of fabric. This arrangement is called a lay plan. In a fully automated factory, the lay plan is created by the computer after the grading process. A light pen is used to move the pattern pieces on the screen so waste is kept to a minimum. This information is stored and can be printed if a small-scale plan of the layout is needed.

Alternatively, a lay plan can be produced manually and, with experience, the process need not be too time-consuming. The pattern pieces are manipulated on the fabric until the best lay-out has been found. The outline of each pattern piece is then traced on to the fabric or marker paper.

Unfortunately, producing a lay plan is not just about achieving the most efficient fit; the **directional properties** of the fabric must also be considered. Pattern pieces usually follow the **grainline** of the fabric but in some instances they should follow the **bias** (see diagram at the top of the next page). Certain fabrics have a nap or pile so that if the fabric is to lie in the same direction, all the pattern pieces must follow that direction. Checks, stripes and other patterns that match must be aligned correctly and require extra fabric.

▼ *The directional properties of a fabric must be considered when producing a lay plan.*

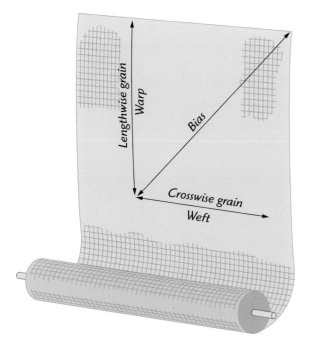

Prototypes

A **prototype** is a model of an idea that is made to see how well it works. A designer may make a paper prototype of a pattern, particularly if the design is complex. The pattern pieces are pinned or stuck in the way the item will be joined. Although paper does not hang like fabric, it is more economical to test and alter a paper pattern than to use fabric.

Clothing designers or tailors making **bespoke** garments may also make prototypes. These are often referred to as toiles. Toiles are usually made out of calico or a similar, cheap fabric. They are often fitted on to a **mannequin**. The mannequin's size can be altered slightly but the client has to try on the finished toile to ensure it fits exactly.

▼ *Computer systems like Gerber's Accumark™ offer a range of facilities such as pattern-making and grading.*

cutting and costing

Preparing to cut

In industry, several layers of fabric are cut at the same time in order to speed up the production process. However, before the pattern pieces can be cut in fabric, a cutting marker has to be made. This is a sheet with all the pieces marked on it and it is used as a guide for the cutting. If clothing manufacturers use an automated system then the cutting marker can be produced by computer.

Next, the fabric must be layered carefully and neatly, ready to be cut. This process is called spreading and is carried out by machines to ensure the fabric lies flat and smoothly. Each layer of fabric is known as a ply, and the number of plies depends on the type of fabric used and the item being produced. After the spreading process, the cutting marker is placed on top of the fabric, ready to guide the cutting.

Identifying the pieces

Using today's technology it is even possible to use machines to identify the pieces of fabric to be cut. The system is set up in two parts: first, information is printed on to adhesive-backed labels; then the labels are automatically placed at the exact location on the fabric. Once the pattern pieces have been cut out they are easily identifiable.

Cutting out

Cutting usually takes place in two stages: first, the pieces are cut roughly to separate them; then each piece is cut out accurately. The type of cutting tool used will depend on the number of layers and type of fabric. Hand shears are used for one or two layers of fabric, but if the pile is any thicker, one of the following machine tools will be needed:

- Straight knives – vertical blades around which a skilled cutter must manipulate the layers of fabric.
- Band knives – blades that also cut vertically, used for precise cutting during the second stage of cutting.
- Circular cutters – used for cutting straight lines and shallow curves; useful during the first stage of cutting.
- Die cutters – an expensive way of cutting fabric because the machine's cutting tools are made to the exact shape of the pattern pieces. For this reason, die cutters are only used for patterns that are likely to remain the same for a long period of time. The cutting tool, or die, is used to stamp out the pattern pieces on a base plate, for example during the production of gloves and ties.

Automated cutting

Fully automated cutting systems are now available, such as the one shown in the picture opposite. They provide accurate, consistent cutting and can also be on a conveyor system to save time. The fabric is cut using sharp, vertical knives with little human intervention.

Marking the spot

Before an item can be sewn together, each piece of fabric must be marked with notches. These indicate the position of features such as darts and also ensure the fabric is situated in exactly the right place. When a large number of items is

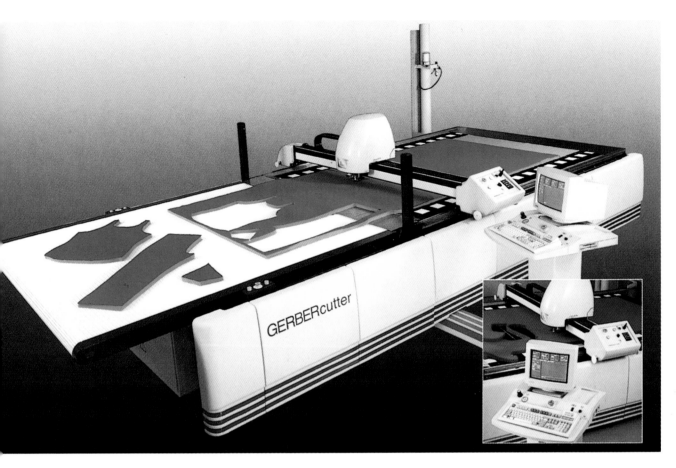

produced the fabric must be marked quickly and accurately, and in a way that will not be visible to the consumer. Various methods are used but one of the most effective is a fluorescent marker that makes dots on the fabric. These dots are only visible under UV (ultraviolet) light, so special UV lamps are placed near the sewing machines. Alternative methods include making small holes or small scorch marks on the fabric.

Counting the cost

When a manufacturer wants to set the price for a textile item, they have to consider a number of factors. They will vary according to the item, but as a general guide the following are taken into account:

- Production costs – these will depend on the complexity of the production,

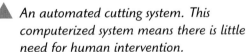

An automated cutting system. This computerized system means there is little need for human intervention.

because the more component parts and the greater the number of operations, the higher the cost of production. The cost of wastage will be calculated here. In addition, the amount of time needed to perform each operation will add to the overall cost.

- Labour costs – not only the number of workers involved but their level of expertise will affect the cost.
- Administration costs – these include all paperwork and value added tax (VAT) as well as any **overheads** such as fuel bills.
- Profit – the amount of profit required will depend on the scale and type of production.

sewing up

Today the majority of sewing machines are electric, which means the process of sewing a textile item can be done quickly and effortlessly. In addition to the common semi-automatic sewing machine, there are automatic and electronic types.

Semi-automatic

Semi-automatic sewing machines are excellent for all straightforward machining. They are controlled using a foot pedal and as well as straight stitch (forward and reverse) they can be adjusted for zig-zag stitch. (If a machine has a swing needle this means the needle can move from side to side to perform a zig-zag stitch.) Both the length and width of the stitch can be adjusted according to the type of fabric, type of sewing and desired effect.

Automatic

Automatic sewing machines have the advantage of automatically adjusting when set to do a particular task. A wider variety of stitch options is also available such as embroidery stitches and automatic buttonholes.

Electronic

Electronic sewing machines have a wide variety of decorative stitches programmed into their memory so the user simply has to choose the right

▼ *In addition to the basic functions, this semi-automatic machine has a numbering system to aid threading; a drop feed lever (located at the back) to lower the teeth for free embroidery and quilting; a one-step buttonholer; and 35 stitch functions.*

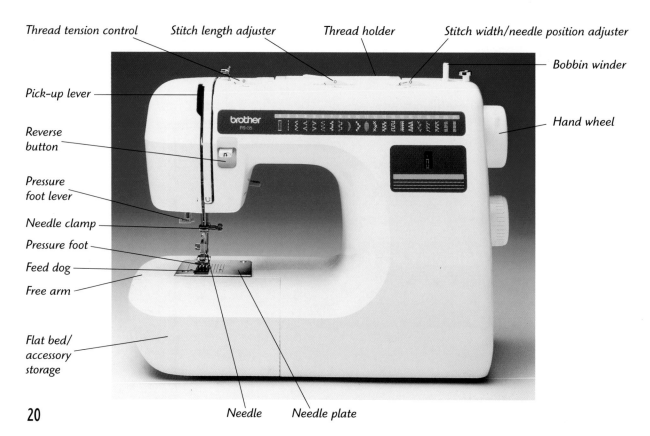

Thread tension control · Stitch length adjuster · Thread holder · Stitch width/needle position adjuster

Pick-up lever

Bobbin winder

Reverse button

Hand wheel

Pressure foot lever

Needle clamp

Pressure foot

Feed dog

Free arm

Flat bed/ accessory storage

Needle · Needle plate

option and the stitch is produced automatically in the correct length and width. Computer disks or cartridges are also available containing a whole range of stitches, pictures, letters, numbers and designs. By inserting the disk or cartridge and choosing an option, the effect will be sewn with no other intervention by the user. If the electronic sewing machine comes with a scanner, original designs can be scanned and saved in the machine's memory.

Machine parts

The picture on the previous page is of a domestic, semi-automatic sewing machine. Although sewing machines vary in their functions (and therefore their price), the basic parts are similar.

Machine needles

All sewing needles have been carefully engineered so the point will not damage the fibres of the fabric. It is important to check machine needles before you sew to ensure they are not bent or blunt from over-use. Unlike sewing needles, machine needles have their eye just above the point.

There are four main categories of machine needles: set points, round points, cutting points and twin needles. Twin needles are two needles joined together so a double row of stitches can be sewn close together and at the same time. You might need them to produce a decorative effect, perhaps with different coloured threads, or to produce a particularly strong seam, for example on a pair of jeans.

Machine stitches

To stitch using a machine, two sets of threads are used. It is important that the **tension** between the two threads is even, otherwise the stitching will look unsightly and may easily undo. The top thread (in the needle) catches the bottom thread (on the bobbin) and the two lock together. However, if the tension at the top is too tight, the bottom thread can be seen on the top of the fabric, and if the tension at the top is too loose, the top thread will appear at the back of the fabric. The diagram below illustrates these variations in tension.

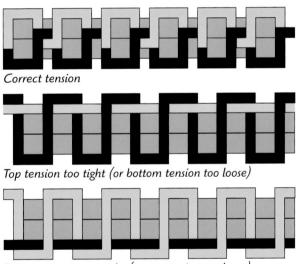

Correct tension

Top tension too tight (or bottom tension too loose)

Bottom tension too tight (or top tension too loose)

After testing a double layer of sample fabric, the top tension can be adjusted, if necessary using the thread tension control (see the photograph opposite). To alter the tension of the bobbin thread, a tiny screw on the outside of the bobbin case can be tightened or loosened very slightly until the correct tension is achieved.

industrial sewing

In order to produce items on a large scale, the textile industry must work quickly and efficiently on construction. The sewing machines used to join fabrics work in a similar way to domestic machines but they tend to be designed for specific jobs. For example, not all machines are flat bed like the domestic sewing machine in the photograph on page 20, although these are used for all sorts of flat sewing. The flat bed provides plenty of space for guiding and turning the fabric.

Industrial machines

To machine sew corners and tight curves, a post bed machine is used. The needle on this type of machine is higher than usual, and there is a post under it. The post enables the machinist to stitch around armholes or corners easily. The cylinder bed machine also stitches at a greater height, and the bed comes out from the front of the machine, like an arm bending around underneath the needle. This allows the machinist to stitch tubular garments like trouser legs and sleeves. A side bed machine has the specific task of sewing edges. Machines with a raised bed carry out specialist tasks like buttonholes, buttons and zips.

Overlockers

Overlockers are used by the textile industry to finish seams, but today domestic versions are available so that anyone can give their products a professional look. The overlocker is a machine that will simultaneously stitch, trim and neaten seams. It can be used with both woven and knitted fabric because the type of stitch used means that it will stretch with the fabric if necessary.

An overlocker may have two, three or four threads and one or two needles; it does not need a bobbin thread. It creates a chain stitch to sew and bind the edge of a seam to prevent it from fraying. A cutting blade trims the seam just before it is overlocked. The distance from the seamline to the edge of the fabric can be adjusted, which enables you to sew different types of textile items. Although overlockers are fiddly to thread, they save time and produce secure seams which can contribute to the overall quality of the end-product.

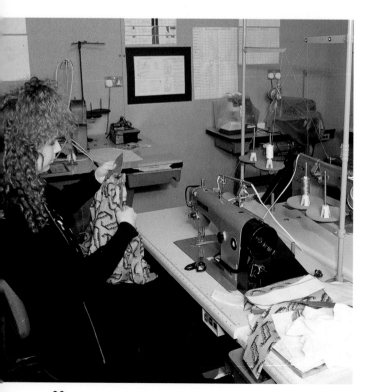

Industrial sewing machines are designed for specific jobs. Speed and efficiency are very important to the textile industry.

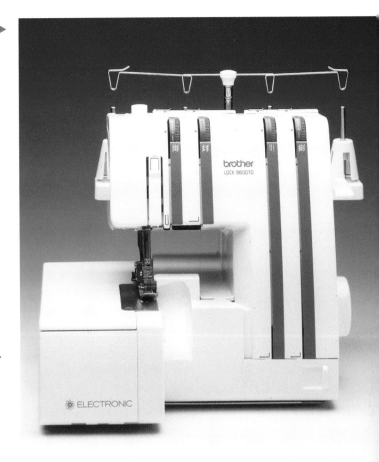

CAM

Computers are not just used in the design of textile items. CAM (**computer-aided manufacture**) is now an important feature of the textile industry. CAM involves computers in the control of equipment; in fact, large companies are likely to use them to control their entire manufacturing process.

Advantages of CAM

The use of CAM has many advantages.

- One person can control an entire range of manufacturing operations with a computer, reducing the number of staff needed.
- Each task is performed exactly the same way every time and the risk of human error is considerably reduced.
- Small changes that are made to the design of a product can be implemented very easily. (This is useful if a **client** has requested a short run of a particular product.)
- When producing textile items using **batch production**, machines have to be re-set after one batch ready for the next batch. By linking the machines to computers, any such changes will occur automatically, saving time, and therefore money, for the company.
- Using computerized machines to perform dangerous jobs, such as those involving harmful chemicals, reduces the risks for textile workers.

Disadvantages of CAM

- Although CAM systems are cheaper to run than employing a large labour force, the set-up costs are expensive.
- If the system should fail for any reason, the company will incur both a loss in production and repair costs.
- Automated systems inevitably mean fewer people are employed, which increases levels of unemployment.

Hand in hand

Generally in the textiles industry the manufacture of a complete product is the result of both CAM and hand operations. Even during **mass production** there may be processes that cannot be carried out by computerized machines. Usually the more that is done by hand, the more expensive an item will be. This is why items produced by **one-off production** are more costly than those that are mass produced.

fabric joining

Seams

Seams are formed when two pieces of fabric are joined together. There are several types of seam, and choosing the most suitable one depends on:

- the fabric you are using (How fine or thick is it? Does it fray? Does it stretch? Does it press easily?)
- the intended location of the seam (Will the seam need to be strong? Is it a design feature? How should it be finished?)

When following commercial patterns, you usually leave a **seam allowance** of 15mm, which is trimmed to 5mm once you have made the seam (although this depends on the seam type). Most seams are held in position with **tacking stitches** before you machine stitch them. Stretch fabrics must be stitched using a stretch stitch or a narrow zig-zag to prevent the thread from breaking as the fabric extends.

Finishing seams

Unless you are using an **overlocker**, most seams will need finishing to prevent fraying. Some seaming techniques, such as the one used for French seams (see opposite), include finishing as part of the process. Other seams need to be finished separately. It is possible to use **pinking shears** to trim and finish a seam, but these will not completely prevent fraying and are only really suitable for non-fraying fabrics such as felt. You can use a zig-zag stitch to finish some seams, as long as the fabric is not so fine that the stitches show through.

Seam types

Flat seam

Flat or plain seams are the common open type of seam, suitable for most fabrics. Place two pieces of fabric together with their *right* sides facing inwards and the edges that you need to sew, exactly on top of one another. Pin the seam, then tack 15mm from the fabric edge. Machine stitch along the tacking using a straight stitch and fasten each end by doing some reverse stitching.

To finish a flat seam on bulky fabric, you press the seam open and trim it to 5mm. You then zig-zag stitch each raw edge and press the seam again. If the seam is particularly long, you can zig-zag stitch the edges first and omit the trimming. To finish a flat seam on less bulky fabric, you trim the seam first and then zig-zag stitch the edges together. You press the seam to one side to create a closed plain seam.

Flat fell seam

A flat fell or double stitched seam is often used for jeans, children's dungarees and outdoor wear because it is a strong method of joining fabric. To make a flat fell seam you place the two pieces of fabric with their *wrong* sides facing and raw edges matching. Pin, tack and sew the seam 15mm from the fabric edge. Press the seam open and then trim one of the seam allowances to 5mm. Fold the other seam allowance in half so the two raw edges meet. Press, pin and tack down the folded edge (raw edges hidden), and finally machine-stitch it in position using a straight stitch.

The flat fell seam does not need finishing because the raw edges are tucked inside. A contrasting colour thread can be used to make a feature of the double seam.

Flat seam

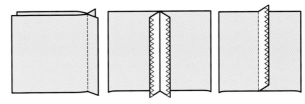

French seam

French seams are similar to flat fell seams because they do not need to be finished and they also require two rows of stitching. To make a French seam, place two pieces of fabric, *wrong* sides together and raw edges matching. Pin, tack and straight-stitch the seam 15mm (or as appropriate) from the raw edge. Press the seam open, then trim both seam allowances to 5mm. Fold the fabric, *right* sides together along the machine line. Pin, tack and machine stitch the seam 5mm from the edges (following the trimmed seam allowance).

Flat fell seam

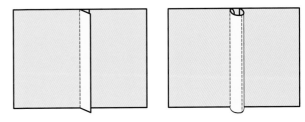

The French seam is particularly suitable for fine fabrics, so it is often used on lingerie, baby clothes and nightwear.

French seam

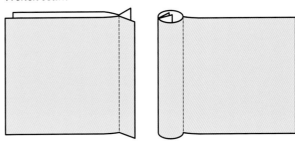

Lapped seam

When joining bulky fabrics such as towelling, you can use a lapped seam to both join and neaten the fabric simultaneously. To make a lapped seam place two pieces of fabric side by side with *right* side upwards and edges overlapping. The overlap is equivalent to a seam allowance so it should measure 15mm. After pinning and tacking, join the seam with two rows of zig-zag, stitched along the two raw edges. Lapped seams are not appropriate for fabrics that fray easily or where the stitching would look unsightly.

Lapped seam

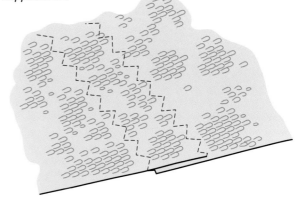

moulding fabric

Knitted items and those made from stretch fabrics will stretch to take up the shape of the article or person they are covering. A swimming costume, a car seat cover and cycle shorts, all give a close fit. A knitted garment will stretch to the shape of a person's body, including a bust or bottom that may stick out! However, for a great deal of textile work a flat fabric has to be made to mould into a three-dimensional shape. To cover the contours of a human body or a piece of furniture, fabric must be carefully cut, eased, manipulated and joined in the correct manner. There are several ways of making a two-dimensional fabric curve and bend to fit a variety of shapes and sizes.

Darts

Darts are most commonly associated with garment construction, but all kinds of textile items require the addition of darts to give them the correct form. A dart is a stitched fold, usually at a seamline, used to shape fabric. A dart placed at the waistline of trousers will reduce the amount of fabric required at the waist in comparison with the amount of fabric needed for the bottom and hips.

Darts are usually triangular and taper to a point at the tip. They must be stitched carefully so they leave a smooth shape on the right side of the product. If the dart does not taper gradually the fabric could stick out at the end of the dart. Darts can be straight or curved. You transfer the markings for a dart from a paper pattern on to the fabric before construction. The pattern is shaped to allow for the extra fabric involved in a dart. After stitching, you press the dart on to the appropriate side, where the triangle of fabric will be least visible and bulky.

In addition to garments, darts are also used in the construction of soft toys, upholstery and some types of hat.

Making darts
To make a dart after having transferred all markings on to the fabric:
- Fold the fabric at the centre of the dart making sure all markings match.
- Pin and press dart in position then tack along machine line. Remove pins.
- Using a straight stitch, machine-stitch the dart carefully, ending it with a fine point. Make sure the stitches are secured by reversing at both ends.
- Remove tacking stitches and press the dart to the appropriate side.

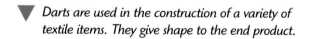

Darts are used in the construction of a variety of textile items. They give shape to the end product.

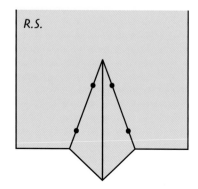

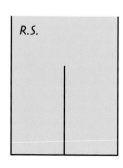

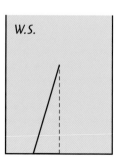

Double darts

Double-pointed darts are used to create curves, perhaps to give shape to a dress that does not have any front seams or fastenings. The two wide ends of the darts meet in the centre and taper to a point at the top and bottom. In the case of a dress, this emphasizes the curve of the waist while allowing more fabric at the bust and hips.

Seams

A seam can be used instead of a dart to give a garment or textile item a certain amount of shape. By joining two pieces of shaped fabric, you can create a curve or a bend. These seams are often used for aesthetic as well as functional reasons, as on the denim jacket pictured here.

Yokes

A yoke is the top section at the front and/or back of some dresses, shirts, blouses, jackets, tops and coats. (The denim jacket shown here has a front yoke.) By separating the top section the fabric attached below can have gathers, pleats, more than one section etc. which can add fullness or shape as appropriate. A yoke does not have to be straight and it can also be in more than one section – for example, on a shirt front.

Although the function of a yoke is to add shape to a garment, the way yokes are used is often dictated by fashion. It has been fashionable to have a yoke in a contrasting fabric or in a different colour. Depending on the desired effect, a yoke can be positioned at the back of a garment, at the front, or both the back and the front.

▲ *This denim jacket illustrates the way seams and yokes can be used to shape a garment.*

shaping fabric

Gather up

The technique of gathering enables you to add fullness to an area of a garment or textile item. Very gentle gathering also allows you to ease a piece of fabric into position, perhaps around a curve like an armhole. Gathering may be purely decorative, to create a frill on a garment or item such as a bag.

Gathering principles

The principle of gathering is the same whether it is carried out by hand or machine. You sew two rows of even stitching to the fabric edge that needs to be gathered, securing each row of stitching at one end only but at opposite ends to one another. This means the fabric can be pulled up from both edges, ensuring an even distribution of gathers. Once the gathered fabric has been attached in the appropriate place, you remove the gathering stitches.

Hand-stitched gathering is time-consuming and you have to take care to ensure the stitches are the same size, otherwise the gathers will be uneven. Machine gathering stitches are usually larger than normal stitches, making it easier to pull up the fabric. As stitches can snap quite easily, it is best to do the gathering slowly and gently.

All tucked up

A tuck is a fold in a fabric. It is either held in position by the seam stitching or each tuck is individually stitched. Tucks are used to create fullness in particular areas such as the waistband of trousers or shorts. Waistband tucks allow for the fact that people usually narrow at the waist so, unless elastic is used, more fabric will be needed below the waistband. Pintucks are very narrow tucks stitched in rows; they are sometimes used at the **neckline** of blouses, below which extra fabric is needed to allow for the bustline.

Making tucks

Tucks are very easy to do, although when they are small and there are many of them, it is important that you do your measuring and sewing accurately. Commercial patterns often indicate tucks using lines, and you have to transfer these markings on to the fabric. Then you fold the fabric from one line to the other and secure it, first by ironing and then by pinning and sewing. You can stitch the tucks across the top or down their length.

When designing textile items with tucks it is important to consider the direction of the tucks, for example, tucks at the waistband are usually folded towards the centre. Extra fabric has to be allowed for tucks, and items containing a lot of tiny pintucks are usually more expensive, due to the added fabric and labour.

Pleats

Pleats are very similar to tucks but they are pressed or machine-stitched into position along the length of the garment or item. Due to the nature of a pleat, they can provide a great deal of fullness and enable a fabric to 'flow'. There are several different types of pleat; the variety and number depends on the design of the textile item.

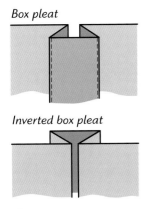
Box pleat

Inverted box pleat

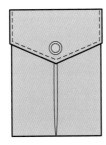
Pleated pocket of a tailored jacket

▲ *Types of pleat.*

A knife pleat is a simple fold in the fabric; the fold can be in either direction. When two knife pleats are placed together in opposite directions, they form a box pleat. When two knife pleats are placed together with the folds of fabric pointing towards one another, the pleat is called an inverted box pleat.

▼ *Pleats in action. These kilts illustrate accordian pleating which gives fabric a great deal of movement.*

When a series of knife pleats are placed together, all facing the same direction, the effect is known as accordion pleating. Pleats are always pressed into position and, for **thermoplastic** materials (e.g. polyester), they can be permanently heat-set. The pleats in some fine fabrics can be edge-stitched to give them a sharper finish. Sometimes pleats are stitched part of the way down, for example, on kilts and other pleated skirts.

A kick pleat is a short pleat at the hem of a skirt. These pleats hang better if the fabric is folded all the way from the waistline but this can sometimes be too bulky, especially for long skirts. In this case the pleat is added as a separate piece of material. Kick pleats are usually stitched at the top, on the right side of the garment, to prevent the pleat from pulling open.

couture millinery

Hats provide an excellent example of manipulating a flat piece of fabric to create a three-dimensional form. This is achieved through cutting and sewing or steaming and moulding, or a combination of the two. Many fabrics can be used in the making of hats – for example, felt, straw, silk, denim, wool, gabardine, cotton and fur. Hats can be mass-produced or they are made to order by a **couture milliner**.

A case study

Katharine Goodison is a couture milliner in London. She designs and makes hats to her **clients'** specifications, mainly for weddings but also for occasions such as horse race meetings or christenings. She has always had an interest in textiles, fashion and design but actually trained and worked as a lawyer for several years before getting involved in the business of hats.

Setting up a business

Katharine enjoyed creating and wearing hats she had designed so, while working as a lawyer, she spent two summers attending millinery courses at the London College of Fashion. Her enthusiasm was such that during each course she not only made twice as many hats as anybody else but wrote copious notes about the other students' hats as well as her own! Gradually friends started requesting hats until eventually she could not keep up with the demand while still working as a lawyer. After producing a detailed business plan, Katharine began to work full time as a couture milliner.

Client consultation

Katharine believes her specialist skill helps to fill a gap in today's fashion market. During the 60s, 70s and 80s the hat industry was at a low ebb but today millinery has become a glamorous art form and consumers are choosing to wear hats more often and with more confidence.

When a client first approaches Katharine, they are invited to her studio for a consultation. This is an important part of the design-and-make process for Katharine, as she has to assess the client's needs in terms of colour, shape, design and overall effect. The client is often looking for a hat to go with a particular outfit, so they bring the outfit to this consultation. Katharine considers her hats to be 'working' hats until they are completely finished because the design often develops while the hat is being created.

Making a hat

All the hats consist of a **crown** and a **brim**. Depending on the design, Katharine makes these two parts separately and joins them afterwards. She uses a combination of moulding and flat pattern work (fabric joined and shaped using seams and darts).

Katharine gets her materials from a range of sources – such as felts from Luton, and straw from the Far East – and the choice very much depends on the client, the season and the expense. She uses a lot of silks, particularly dupion, as it provides a huge choice of colours, although Katharine will dye her fabrics to ensure an exact match for her clients. Trimmings range from furs and flowers to buttons and bows.

▲ Couture milliner, Katharine Goodison with a selection of her creative hats.

The straw fabric Katharine purchases has been semi-moulded and cut, so it has the appearance of a soft, unfinished hat. She uses this to create moulded hats. To mould the crown and brim of the hat, Katharine uses wooden blocks of various shapes. By applying heat and water to the fabric, she can pull and manipulate the hat into the desired shape. The hat is held in position with pins while the fabric dries, and it usually shrinks a little in the process. Once it has dried she applies stiffeners and glue to the fabric and inserts wires to help 'persuade' the fabric to retain its shape. Katharine always stiches the crown and brim together by hand, and may put **petersham** around the inside edge of the crown to make it more comfortable to wear.

The client returns to Katharine's studio once the basic hat has been made to ensure a correct fit. If necessary, Katharine then drapes the hat with a variety of trimmings to help the client decide on the final look.

Sinamay

Sinamay is the latest fabric to be used for making hats. It is thought to have been introduced into millinery by Philip Treacy, British Accessory Designer of the Year in 1991, 1992 and 1993. Sinamay is woven from banana fibre in the Philippines and has been used by florists and gardeners for years. It is lighter and more versatile than straw, can be purchased in sheet form and dyes beautifully.

sleeve shapes

When knitted and sewn garments are made, the sleeves are either produced separately and then sewn on to the main body of the garment, or they are produced all-in-one, as part of the garment. Separate sleeves give the finished article more shape but they also involve more skill during the design and manufacture.

Basic sleeves

Both sewn and knitted garments have the choice of three basic sleeve types: set-in, raglan and kimono. However, a huge variety of sleeves can be created using these three basic types. The shape of a sleeve can dictate the look of the whole garment, so it is very important that it is designed with both the function and the style of the garment in mind.

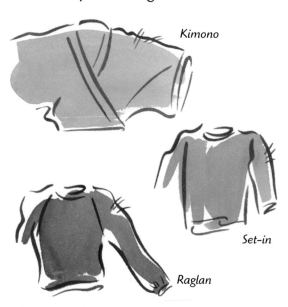

Kimono

Set-in

Raglan

Set-in sleeves

A basic set-in sleeve sits on the edge of the shoulder and fits comfortably around the armhole. It is very important that the top edge of the sleeve is shaped to fit perfectly into the armhole space.

The design and look of a set-in sleeve may be varied by adding fullness to the top of the sleeve. This may be achieved with gathers, pleats and darts and by allowing extra fabric and shape at the sleeve head. Puff sleeves are an example of a sleeve with a full head. In addition, shoulder pads can be incorporated into set-in sleeves (and at shoulder of the bodice) in order to give the garment height. This style was particularly popular in the 1980s and was associated with women and 'power dressing'.

A further variation is to drop the shoulderline of a set-in sleeve. In this case the armhole edge of the bodice is extended while the curve of the sleeve head is made less deep. The sleeve can also be an extension to a yoke so the top of the sleeve continues over the shoulder, up to the neck.

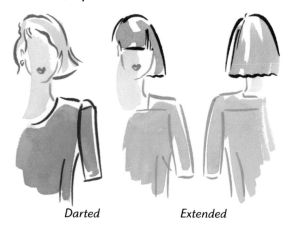

Darted

Extended

Raglan sleeves

A raglan sleeve can be identified in a garment where the sleeve seam extends from below the arm to the **neckline**. These sleeves provide fewer opportunities for variation but the shape of clothes can be altered by changing the seamline of the sleeve. A deep raglan, for example, has a lower seamline than a classic raglan. Shoulders can be squared off by adjusting the shape of the raglan pattern and top stitching also gives emphasis to the raglan shape. A raglan sleeve can be prepared as one piece of fabric, or it can be made from two or more which will create seams along the length of the sleeve.

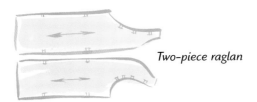

Two-piece raglan

Kimono sleeves

Kimono style sleeves are easy to construct because they are formed all-in-one with the body. The effect is a wide sleeve that hangs beneath the armhole and is shaped by the folds of the fabric. A kimono sleeve may be varied with careful shaping of the lower seam. A batwing sleeve, for example, has a curve that is more shallow than the classic kimono. The curve can also be replaced with a square-shaped sleeve. By adding seams to a kimono shape, it can be given a completely different look, such as the kimono with a yoke shown in the illustration. A cap sleeve is based on a classic kimono shape because it does not have a seam to join it to the armhole.

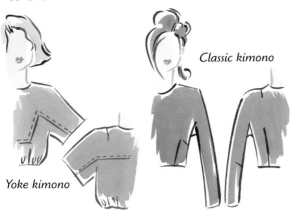

Yoke kimono
Classic kimono

More shapes

Of course, many of the styles mentioned above can be combined with each other and all sleeves can be varied in their length and width. The diagram below shows the main lengths used for sleeves.

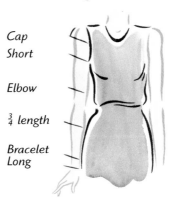

Cap
Short

Elbow

$\frac{3}{4}$ length

Bracelet
Long

In addition, sleeves may flare out to the desired length or they may be tailored to fit closely to the arm. Long sleeves may be shaped with a small seam at the elbow, especially jacket sleeves, to allow the arm to bend without straining the fabric. Whether or not a sleeve is to have a cuff must be taken into account in the design process because the lower part of the sleeve will need to be shaped accordingly. Some sleeves, such as shirt sleeves, may have a back seam while others may be given a very formal appearance using a raised seam along the front edge of the sleeve.

Raised seam

Necklines

When designers design garments such as shirts, tops and dresses, the **neckline** is an important consideration. In some cases it can be the main feature of the item. The choice of neckline will largely depend on the function of the garment.

Collars

The designer may include a collar – some necklines need a collar while others do not. A collar is the part of a garment that is formed around the neck. A basic T-shirt does not have a collar, nor do **cowl** or **slash** necklines (see below).

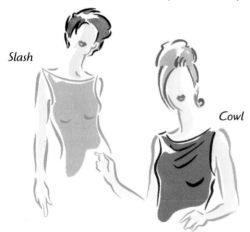

Slash

Cowl

By combining different necklines and types of collar, a huge range of styles can be generated. Naturally fashion plays an important role in dictating the shape of collars for any particular season, but it is quite amazing how a garment can be totally transformed just by changing the collar design.

As a guide to the different styles of collar, they can be divided into the following categories: flat collars, standing collars, collars cut with the garment and collars with revers.

Flat collars

Examples of flat collars include Peter Pan, sailor and Eton collars. The collar lies flat against the garment hence the name. It is attached at the neckline seam. They are relatively quick and easy to assemble and can be varied by using contrasting fabrics. They may also vary in shape and size.

Peter Pan

Eton

Sailor

(front)

(back)

Flat collars can be made into frilly collars by gathering or pleating the fabric. A **jabot** is an example of a long collar that hangs in folds. These were particularly popular during the 1920s.

Standing collars

A shirt collar is an example of a standing collar as the collar is attached to a separate 'stand' or band around the neckline of the garment. The collar can vary in shape and size and can consist of the stand on its own, as in a mandarin collar. A grandad collar also consists of the stand but unlike the mandarin, it has a fastening at the front.

Mandarin

Grandad

Collars cut with the garment

These collars also lie flat on the garment but they are not joined to the neckline; they are cut as part of the garment. Once complete, the collar is folded (as in the roll collar) or pressed on to the outside of the garment. These collars are particularly useful if the design does not require a collar at the back of the neck (as in the rever front collar, for example.)

Roll

Rever front

Collars with revers

A rever is the turned back front edge at the neckline of a garment. They are made from two sections, some joined, others not. The top section is the collar and the lower section the rever. Tailored jackets usually have revered collars.

Classic tailored jacket collar

Cuffs

A cuff is used to give a neat finish to a sleeve, or sometimes a trouser leg. A cuff can also serve the purpose of gathering together excess fabric if the sleeve or trouser leg is quite wide. An unfastening cuff allows the garment to be taken off easily but a good fit when the garment is being worn. Once again fashion plays a big part in deciding whether a garment has fullness in the arms and legs, and whether this should be drawn in by a cuff. The size of a cuff can also vary according to the current trends.

Cuffs that fasten usually have buttons, but press studs or even Velcro are possible alternatives. Other types of cuff are large enough for a hand or foot to pass through without being unfastened or are able to stretch as in elasticated and ribbed cuffs. A cuff may be single or double, the latter having sufficient length to fold back over itself. Shaped and frilled cuffs are often designed quite long so that they fall on to the back of the hand.

fasten up

Button up

Buttons are the common means of fastening textile items, especially clothes. They are available in all shapes and sizes, and can enhance the decorative value of the end-product. Buttons can be made from a wide range of materials including wood, metal, nylon, polyester, leather, glass and pearl. Some buttons are covered with fabric that matches or complements the textile item. Generally speaking, buttons are either flat with holes in the centre so they can be attached, or they have a shank, which is a solid loop underneath the button that provides an anchor for attachment.

Buttonholes

Most buttons are designed to be used with buttonholes. These can be made by hand or machine, and must be strong enough to withstand pressure if the button pulls against them. Buttonholes can be stitched in contrasting thread and shaped at the edges to give a decorative finish.

Toggles

Toggles are a specific type of button. They are often made from wood and have an elongated shape; they are used on duffle coats and children's wear. Toggles can be used with buttonholes but they are often fastened with a 'frog'. This is a loop of cord or leather through which the toggle can pass. Although not a particularly strong method for fastening, the 'frog and toggle' can look attractive and is easy to manipulate, especially for children.

Snap shut

The original snap fastener has developed and diversified. Manufacturers now make gripper fasteners, tack buttons, rivets and burrs. Snap fasteners are used for a wide range of items including sports clothes, backpacks, even diving equipment. They provide a safe, non-scratch fastening which is particularly suitable for children's garments. There are even some designed to government specifications for military use.

Gripper snap fasteners are ideal for infantwear because they are smooth and hazard-free for children, and are easy for parents to manipulate as they dress the child. They come in a wide range of colours. Heavier fabrics such as denim often have tack buttons, rivets and burrs. Tack buttons serve mainly as fasteners but rivets and burrs are used for reinforcement and decoration. They often incorporate logos such as the designer labels seen on rivets on jeans.

Hook and eye

Hooks and eyes or hooks and bars are used as a simple fastening, perhaps on skirts or trousers, and often at the top of a small zip. They are not generally strong enough to be used on their own and, as they are very fiddly to attach, not often found on **mass produced** textile items. However, as a secondary fastening they can be very discreet because they are small and placed on the inside of a garment. The hook, eye and bar are made from metal or nylon and are attached by stitching around the little loops at their edges.

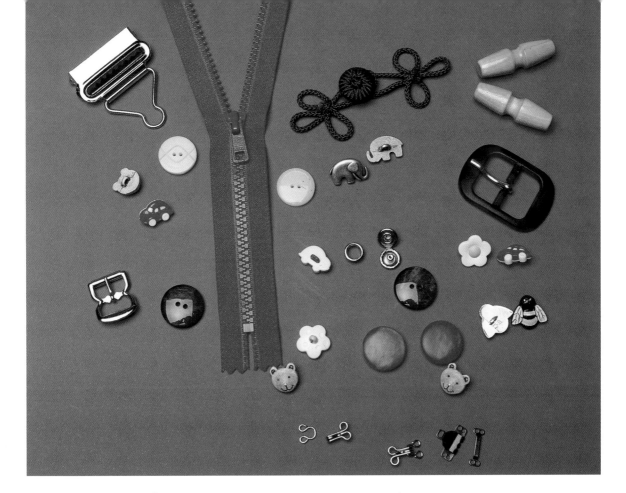

A collection of fastenings.

Lacing together

Some textile items are fastened in a very decorative way using eyelets and laces. The laces are threaded through the eyelet holes and fastened at the bottom. The eyelets can be made from metal, in which case a machine punches the hole and secures the eyelet in place. Or they can be cut and stitched like buttonholes. The type of material used for the laces will depend on the item but they could be fabric, ribbon, leather or cord. Sometimes laces and eyelets are used on garments for purely aesthetic reasons. In the past they were used a lot as a means of fastening, for example, on corsets and dresses.

Ribbons and bows

Knots and bows have been used to fasten clothes for many years. They can be made to look attractive as well as serve a purpose, for example, a sash around a bride's dress can be tied as an eye-catching bow. Ribbons and ties have the advantage of being easy to fasten as well as easy to attach to textile items. However, they are not very secure so they are not often used on items that are likely to undergo heavy handling. Cushion and chair covers might be tied on so that they can be removed easily for washing. Simple garments such as kimonos, aprons and bathrobes are often tied at the waist so they can be taken on and off without effort.

Zips

Zips play an important role in the fastening of many textile items so the following two pages have been devoted to them.

zip it up – a case study

YKK

YKK is one of the leading manufacturers of zip fasteners. They were established in 1966 and YKK (UK) Ltd. was the first Japanese company with a manufacturing unit in the UK. Their head office is in London while their manufacturing centre is in Runcorn, Cheshire. They also have regional Customer Service Centres. YKK now produce a variety of fasteners, in **bespoke** and standard ranges, for both fashion and industry. In addition to zippers, they produce hook and loop fasteners, jeans buttons, press fasteners, rivets and plastic and metal buckles.

How zips work

A zip consists of two edges of teeth attached to a fabric tape and a slider. As the slider is drawn along the length of the zip, the teeth from one edge slot between the teeth from the other edge. The zip cannot be pulled apart and remains secure until the slider is pulled back across the teeth, reversing the process. A garment or textile item has a zip attached along the edge of the tape. Concealed zips have the teeth turned on to the inside of the garment so that they are not visible from the outside. A visible zip may be found on a jacket or sports bag. The tape used with zips comes in an assortment of colours so that it will blend with the fabric. The teeth of nylon zips are also coloured.

Heads or tails?

There are different types of zip for different functions. For example, a head to head zip does not have a top to the zip. It has two sliders that are drawn towards one another. These zips are often used on suitcases and holdalls and the two zips are closed together and secured with a small padlock. Open-ended zips are used for items such as jackets that need to be opened completely. In this case, the slider is pulled down the length of the zip and one edge of the zip is taken out of the bottom 'box'. A head to tail zip is one that does not open at the bottom. The slider is pulled down the zip but it stops at the bottom. These zips are used on trousers, jeans, skirts and shorts. Continuous chain zips are used to speed up garment manufacture. Each side of the zip is joined to the appropriate side of the clothing. When the two sides of the garment are sewn together the zip is fully incorporated.

Sliders

Zips come in a range of materials, colours and sizes but they are basically functional items. However, by adding an eye-catching slider, zips can also be made to look decorative. YKK provide a wide choice of 'fashion sliders' in nickel plate, antique brass, golden brass and enamel in addition to the more usual metal and nylon. The range also includes sliders with leather tabs attached.

Heavy or light?

As garments and textile items are made from a whole array of different fabrics, so zips must come in a choice of weights and sizes. A heavy metal zip would be inappropriate for a soft, lightweight skirt but it would be suitable for a chunky knitted jacket. YKK zips come in three weights for the fashion industry: heavy-, medium- and light-weight. Their light-weight zips are often, but not exclusively, nylon and they are the closed-end variety. These zips are available on knitted or woven tape.

Medium-weight zips are available in metal, aluminium alloy and moulded plastic. They are stronger than the light-weight zips and therefore have a wider range of end-uses. The zips may be closed or open-ended, continuous or double-ended and come with a variety of different sliders. The heavy-weight range includes all the zips mentioned for the medium-weight but there are also those with specific functions – for example, zips that have more than one slider, and tape that is water-repellant, for use in the manufacture of tents.

Fire-retardant

YKK also manufacture specialized fire-retardant zips. These are metal fasteners attached to tape made using Nomax® yarns, which are flame-retardant. These zips are tested in accordance with British Standards (BS 5438).

Latest designs

In addition to its range of zips, YKK produce rivets for jeans and snap fasteners in a range of metals. They also manufacture a hook and loop fastener for a variety of applications, from clothing and accessories to industrial, automotive and aerospace items.

▼ *Zips are basically functioning items but they can also have a decorative appeal.*

Nomax® is a registered trade mark of Dupont.

fastenings from nature

Viscose rayon was originally known as artificial silk because, although it is a synthetic product, it has many of the qualities of silk which comes from a natural source. A silkworm produces a continuous filament of liquid silk, forced out from two glands in its head. The thread is used to spin a cocoon around itself so that it can remain undisturbed as it becomes a chrysalis and finally a moth. By studying the actions of a silkworm, scientists developed the spinneret – which consists of many minute holes through which a liquid is forced – for use in the production of synthetic fibres.

This illustrates the way scientists have borrowed ideas from nature and used them in textiles. Another equally compelling example is that of Velcro®.

The story of Velcro®

Velcro® was invented by a Swiss engineer called George DeMaestral. While out walking his dog in the woods, he noticed cockle-burs sticking to his socks and trousers and his dog's fur. DeMaestral decided to investigate this simple act of nature. By examining the burs under the microscope, he discovered they were covered in tiny hooks. The hooks from the burs were linking with the loops from the fabric of his clothes and the fur on his dog.

A bur is the seedcase of a plant or flower, and nature provides it with hooks so that it can cling to animal fur and so distribute its seeds as widely as possible. It is one of nature's survival mechanisms.

The Swiss engineer decided to copy nature and eventually designed a unique system of fastening, **patenting** his design in 1955. Velcro® is now the trademark for this fastening. The name comes from two French words, *velours* meaning velvet and *crochet* meaning hook.

Contemporary Velcro® is made from nylon and consists of two tapes: one is covered with thousands of tiny hooks; the other with thousands of tiny loops. When the two strips are pressed together the hoops snag and fasten in the opposing loops. The attachment is amazingly strong and is further strengthened by vibration and pressure. However, the hooks can be disengaged from the loops simply by pulling the two strips apart.

Using Velcro®

Velcro® was originally seen as a revolutionary form of fastening but today it is so widespread it is more or less taken for granted. Its benefits are by no means confined to the clothing industry, as it can also be found in the electronics, aircraft, aerospace, furnishing, computer, audio/video and film industries! A less obvious use for Velcro® is the attachment of display material for exhibition in schools, libraries, businesses etc.

Simple but effective

For many people, tying shoe laces or fastening buckles can be tricky but today a great deal of footwear, particularly sports and leisurewear, can be fastened quickly and easily with Velcro®. Specialist

▲ Velcro® highly magnified.

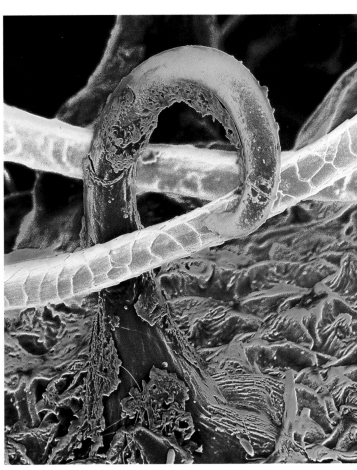

▼ A bur, the seed case of a plant or flower – a simple act of nature inspired the invention of Velcro®.

sports items such as cycle gloves or cricket pads are also easier to manipulate with a 'hook and loop' fastening. Medical devices like surgical collars and splints are more user-friendly with the aid of Velcro®.

Advantages of Velcro®

The versatility of Velcro® is one of its main advantages. The strips of tape can be cut to any size or shape and will not fray. It can be attached to most other materials either by sewing, sticking, stapling or moulding. As Velcro® is made from nylon it has durability and, when used on garments, can easily outlive the fabric! In addition, Velcro® can be washed, dry cleaned and sterilized; it can withstand ironing up to 163°C and although it is only 50 per cent effective when wet, it will return to 100 per cent effectiveness once it is dry.

Testing Velcro®

When testing Velcro® during manufacture it has to be ripped apart and reclosed many times to ensure it will have a long life while remaining completely efficient. Industrial strength Velcro® may undergo tests that open and close it as many as 10,000 times. When closed it is also tested with weights to ensure it will not come undone under pressure.

textile project: hat

Designing and making a hat is an excellent way to illustrate how a flat piece of fabric can be made into a three-dimensional form.

The basic hat pieces shown here are suitable for adapting to make a hat with a **brim**, such as a sunhat, or a hat with a peak, such as a baseball cap. The method used to create a three-dimensional item is to make the **crown** out of segments of fabric, the number and shape of which can vary depending on the look you are hoping to achieve.

▲ *Examples of some hats available today.*

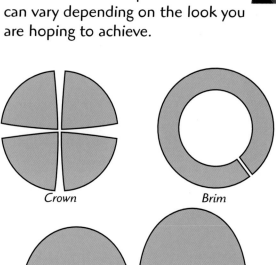

Crown

Brim

Peaks

Developing ideas

Start by looking around at other people, in clothes shops and catalogues. Get a feel for the type of hats already available. Look in fabric shops at the type of fabric and range of colours on offer. Try to think ahead – if another season is about to begin, what are the new colours for that season? If it is springtime now, why not make a hat ready for the summer?

Or, make a baseball cap that will be useful all year round. Sketch all your ideas and **annotate** them with notes about fabric types and construction methods. Refine and improve the ideas you like best and those you think will work well. Add colour and detail to your sketches as they develop.

How are hats made?

Now think carefully about the construction of hats. Which of your designs would be suitable to make? You will need to consider the shape and number of pattern pieces and how they would be joined together. If possible, **disassemble** an old hat, similar in shape to your own design, and work out how it was constructed. Although the crown of a manufactured hat is probably lined, you need not worry about lining yours. However, the brim or peak is likely to be made using two layers of fabric. These will be joined at the outside edge first and then attached to the crown of the hat. Tape or **petersham** can be sewn on to the inside for comfort and to hide any raw edges. You may also notice **interfacing** on a manufactured hat. This helps to reinforce garments and is particularly useful on a brim or peak because it can stiffen the fabric. Very often the brim or peak is top-stitched too.

Using your best design idea, sketch all the two-dimensional pattern pieces needed to make the hat. The next task is to join the pieces of paper to test how well they fit together. You can adjust the pattern to fit your head after you have worked out how the hat will be constructed. Remember the final pattern will need to include a seam allowance of 15mm. Glue or pin the pattern pieces together. Make notes about any alterations and the most suitable way in which to join the separate pieces.

Making a prototype

Once you are happy that the pieces fit together successfully, you will need to make some adjustments to ensure a snug fit. If possible, make up your **prototype** hat (or at least the crown) using some old or cheap fabric to check the size. When preparing the pattern pieces of the correct size, do not forget to add 15mm to each edge.

Use your pattern pieces to work out how much fabric you will need and to minimize wastage, then cut out the fabric using your prepared pattern. Make sure the pieces all lie in the same direction, following the **grainline**. Take care if using

contrasting colours or fabric to ensure that they are facing the correct way.

Making up your hat

Next, using your notes, you can begin constructing your hat. It probably makes most sense to join the segments of the crown first and then add the brim or peak. The lower edge of a cap is finished either by pressing it under and stitching it down, or by adding tape to the edge then pressing and stitching it under. A crown and brim can be machine-stitched using one layer of the brim then turned and stitched on the outside, or attached in one go by machine-stitching them on to the outside.

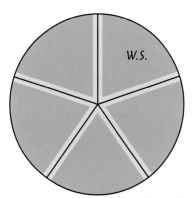

Segments of a crown joined together

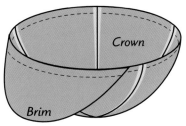

The brim can be attached to the crown in one go and the raw edges pressed under

Once the hat has been constructed, you may choose to decorate it with stitching, buttons, chains, lace, cord, buckles, sequins, flowers, embroidery etc.

resources

Books

The following books are useful for students studying GCSE Design and Technology:

Design & Make It! Textiles Technology Alex McArthur, Carolyn Etchells, Tristram Shepard	Stanley Thornes 1997
Examining Textiles Technology Anne Barnett	Heinemann Educational 1997
Fashion Design and Product Development Harold Carr and John Pomeroy	Blackwell Science 1992
Textiles and Technology (UK edition) Adapted by Margaret Beith	Cambridge University Press 1997
Textiles Technology Alison Bartle and Bernie O'Connor	Causeway Press 1997

The following book is useful for more detailed information on construction techniques:

Vogue/Butterick Step-by-Step Guide to Sewing Techniques (Third edition)	Butterick Publishing Company 1998

I.C.T.

www.craftscouncil.org.uk/exhib.htm
Provides details of forthcoming arts and crafts events throughout the country

www.textile-toolkit.org.uk
Includes news, competitions, details of events and a chat forum for students; there is also a CD-ROM available for use as a teaching aid for GCSE textiles

www.worldtextile.com
Publishes a variety of textile-related journals

Places to visit

Luton Museum and Art Gallery
Wardown Park
Luton LU2 7HA
(Tel no: 01582 546722)
This museum has a nationally important collection related to hats and the hat industry, as well as other exhibits

The Victoria and Albert Museum
Cromwell Road
South Kensington
London SW7 2RL
(Tel no: 020 7942 2000)
Textile exhibitions and Crafts Council shop

The Design Museum
28 Shad Thames
London SE1 2YD
Exhibits focus on design evolution in the 20th century

Contacts

The British Hat Guild
The Business Centre
Kimpton Road
Luton LU2 0LB
(Tel no: 01582 702345; Fax: 01582 702350)
The recognized body for the hat industry; it is an organization to which anyone involved with hats can belong. It provides information to its members on seasonal forecasts of fashion colours, sources of supply lists as well as business information

Scovill Fasteners (UK) Ltd.
Scovill Works
157 Nottingham Road
Old Basford
Nottingham NG6 0FU
(Tel no: 0115 979 1655)
A company that produces press fasteners and speciality closures for the international textile market. They can customize logos using CAD systems and incorporate them on to their fastenings for customers who want personalized garments

YKK (UK) Ltd.
Head Office
61 Central Street
London EC1V 8AN
(Tel no: 020 7253 2077)
Suppliers of a wide range of zips and other fasteners to manufacturers and retailers. They have a number of regional Customer Service Centres

The Crafts Council
44a Pentonville Road
London N1 9BY
(Tel no: 020 7278 7700)
Provides up-to-date information about art and crafts exhibitions and shows; also produces a magazine called Crafts, available on subscription

glossary

annotate add written information to a sketch or label a drawing

batch production the production of garments in batches; for example, a batch of white football shorts followed by a batch of blue ones

bespoke made-to-measure (tailored) method of clothing production; a labour-intensive method, often used in suit production

bias runs diagonally across the fabric's weave and is where the fabric has some stretch; bias binding is a tape made from fabric cut on the bias

block pattern basic pattern shapes that are adapted by the pattern maker to create the specific shape and detail required by the designer

brim outer rim of a hat

British Standards Institute professional organization that decides which tests must be applied to which textile products and sets the standards for the tests

client person or company for whom work is being done

colourways the same design shown in different colours

Computer-aided design (CAD) software used by textile and clothing industry to aid designers

Computer-aided manufacturer (CAM) software used by textile and clothing industry to control machinery during manufacture

couture short for 'haute couture' (see below)

cowl type of neckline that hangs loosely around the neck; often seen on jumpers and blouses

crown top part of a hat, attached to the brim

design brief short statement about the intended use of the product to be designed

directional properties aspects of a fabric's surface that relate to the direction in which the fibres lie, due to the fabric's construction. Fabrics with directional properties include fur, velvet and sateen

disassemble taking apart a garment or textile item in order to find out about its construction

grainline direction in which the yarns travel in a fabric

haute couture French term meaning high-quality clothes, designed and made for a very limited market; sometimes shortened to 'couture'

interfacing fine material used to support certain areas of a garment or textile item. Interfacing is likely to be used inside collars, cuffs and waistbands

jabot frilly neckline that extends down the front of a dress or shirt

mannequin life-size dummy or model used to display clothes

mass production production of clothes and textiles items on a large scale

milliner someone who makes hats

nap forms when the surface of a fabric is raised by brushing; the nap (and pile) lie in one direction so all pattern pieces must be cut following the same direction

neckline the outline formed by the edge of a garment at the neck

need term used to describe something that consumers need (product/service), where there is a gap in the market

notions often seen on commercial patterns to indicate components other than fabric required to make the product, e.g. thread, zip, buttons, bias binding etc.

one-off production production of unique items; they usually involve a lot of time and skill to produce and are relatively expensive to buy; also called 'job production'

overheads running costs incurred by a business, for example rent of premises, fuel bills etc.

overlocker machine that will simultaneously stitch, trim and neaten seams

patent a form of registration showing that a person owns the sole right to a new product or process; it has to be applied for

petersham stiff tape used to support areas of garments and textile items, for example, around the brim of a hat

pinking shears scissors with zig-zag blades used to cut seam allowances and temporarily prevent fraying

prototype model of a design idea, used to test its suitability for production

seam allowance amount of fabric allowed to create a seam; usually 15mm

slash type of neckline; the neck is created within the top seam so the neckline is completely straight; often seen on t-shirts

storyboards board covered with pictures, sketches, swatches etc. used to create a story or feeling about a product to be designed

tacking stitches used to hold fabric in place while it is being sewn; also used to check the fit of a garment before it is sewn; cheap tacking thread is used as the stitches are removed afterwards

tailor's chalk used to mark fabric; often flat with a sharp edge for marking fine lines; easily removed with a brush

tension force applied to the top and bottom thread of a sewing machine; the two should be even for perfect stitching

thermoplastic a property of some (synthetic) fabrics enabling them to soften on heating and harden after cooling

tracing wheel used in conjunction with carbon tracing paper, it marks the surface of a fabric with patterns (series of dots)

virtual reality when something has the appearance of being real but in fact is a computer generated reality

index

batch production 16, 23
bespoke production 17, 38
body measurements 10
British Standards Institute (BSI) 11
buttonhole shears 12
buttonholes 36
buttons 35, 36

clothing sizes 11
collars 9, 34–5
    flat collars 34
    jabot 34
    with revers 35
    roll collars 35
    standing collars 35
colourways 5, 6, 14
computer technology
    computer-aided design (CAD) 5, 6–7
    computer-aided manufacture (CAM) 23
    pattern making 11, 16
    sewing machines 21, 23
cuffs 9, 35
cutting fabric 8, 9, 18
    automated cutting 18, 19
    cutting tools 18
cutting marker 18

darts 9, 18, 26–7, 32
    double-pointed darts 27
design brief 4
design ideas 5, 42
design plans 4
disassembly 5, 8, 9, 42

fabric shears 12, 18
fabrics
    bias 16, 17
    cutting 8, 9, 18
    directional properties 16–17
    grainline 16, 17, 43
    nap 15, 16
fastenings 9, 36–41

gathers 9, 27, 28, 32

hats 30–1, 42–3
haute couture 11, 30–1
hooks and eyes/hooks and bars 36

interfacing 15, 43
irons and ironing boards 13

knitted garments 26

laces and eyelets 37
lay planning 11, 16

mannequins 13, 17
mass production 11, 16, 23, 36
measuring 10–11

necklines 28, 32, 34
    cowl neckline 34
    slash neckline 34
    see also collars
needles
    sewing machines 21
    sizes 12
notchers 12

one-off production 11, 16, 23
overlocker 22, 23, 24

pattern makers 16
patterns 11
    block patterns 11, 16
    commercial patterns 14–15
    fabric information and quantities 15
    industrial pattern making 16–17
    lay plans 11, 16
performance fibres and fabrics 7
pinking shears 12, 24
pleats 9, 27, 28–9, 32
    accordion pleating 29
    box pleats 29
    kick pleats 29
    knife pleats 29
pressing garments 13, 29
production costs 19
prototypes 7, 17, 43

ribbons, ties and bows 37

safety testing 7, 39
scissors and shears 12, 18, 24
seams 24–5, 27
    finishing 22, 24
    flat fell seam 24–5
    flat seam 24

French seam 24, 25
    lapped seam 25
    seam allowances 24
sewing machines 20–3
    automatic 20
    electronic 20–1
    flat bed machines 20, 22
    industrial machines 22
    needles 21
    overlockers 22, 23, 24
    semi-automatic 20
    tension 21
sewing pins 12–13
shape 8, 9, 26
shaping fabric 9, 26–9
sinamay 31
sleeve board 13
sleeve shapes 32–3
    cap sleeves 33
    kimono sleeves 32, 33
    puff sleeves 32
    raglan sleeves 32–3
    set-in sleeves 32
snap fasteners 36
snippers 12
stitch cutter 12
storyboards 5

tacking stitches 24, 26
three-dimensional form 8
toggles 36
toiles 17
tools and equipment 12–13
tucks 28
    pintucks 28

Velcro® 35, 40–1
virtual gloves 7
virtual reality 7

working drawings 5

yokes 27

zip fasteners 37, 38–9